Earth

ENVIRONMENT
COLLECTION FOR KIDS

Israel Felzenszwalb · David Palatnik

Earth

J
55~d
Felzens
2013

Illustrations by
David Palatnik

4

Hello, nice to meet you!
I am EARTH. I appeared a very,
very, very, very, very long time ago,
together with the stars.

And a very long time ago as well,
I formed the PLANET EARTH. At that time I was
very hot and soft, and I was called MAGMA.

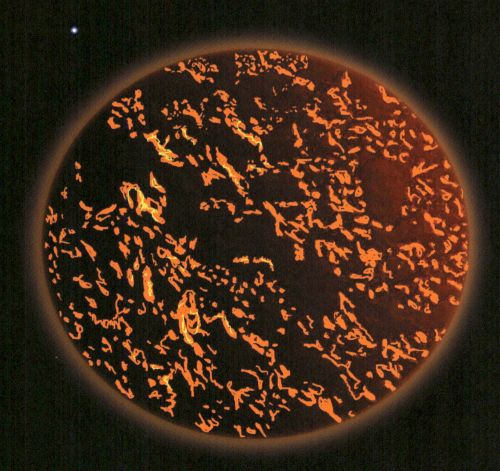

Then my skin, which is called the EARTH'S CRUST, slowly cooled down and hardened. Then came the oceans and the continents, where there are countries and cities.

It was a very good thing that the Earth's crust cooled down, because then I could take DIFFERENT FORMS.

Lava

Rock

Fertile soil

Sand

Clay

When I come out of the mouth of a VOLCANO I am called LAVA, and I am RUNNY and VERY HOT! Later I dry and harden and my colour becomes dark.

VOLCANOES are like CHIMNEYS linking the hot interior of the Earth with its surface.

When the Earth's crust had cooled down, mountains were formed and I was called ROCK. In the form of STONES or POWDER, I can be used for many things.

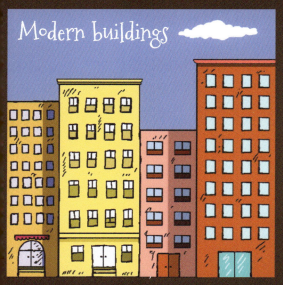
Modern buildings

Sports

Paving stones

Decoration

Utensils

Art

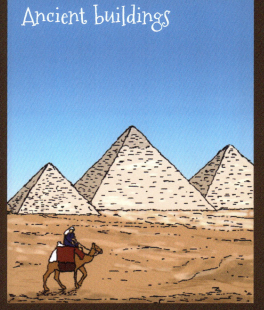
Ancient buildings

Hygiene

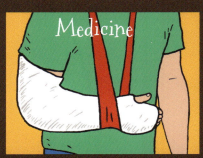
Medicine

I may also appear in the form of CLAY:
other names for this are MUD or
CERAMIC, and it has many uses.

Pots, vases and other objects

Building bricks and tiles

Birds can use me to make a nest

Did you know that some parts of the space shuttle were made of ceramic?

Image based on photo from NASA (North American Space Agency)

Face packs

Sculptures

Wow!!!

If you have ever been to the beach you know me very well. There I'm called SAND! In this form I show up in many other places as well and I can be very useful!

In ancient times an hourglass was used to tell the time.

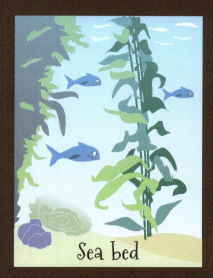

Sea bed

Beach

Did you know that glass is made of sand?

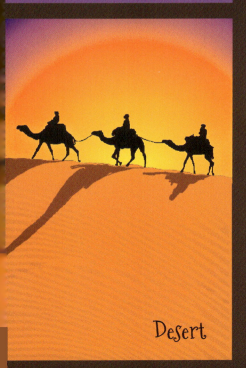

Desert

Where crabs make their houses

Wow!!

When I take the form of fertile soil, I'm used to grow all kinds of plants and I also provide a home for many creatures.

But let me tell you about the problem
that worries me most: GARBAGE!
The whole planet and I are getting
too DIRTY, too POLLUTED!

Let me explain: in addition to all the other things I have told you about, I can also TRANSFORM anything that falls on top of me and STAYS THERE FOR SOME TIME!

For instance, leaves, branches, fruits or seeds that fall from plants.

Or the poo of animals and birds, their fur or feathers and even their bodies when they die.

All this I can TRANSFORM into FERTILISER, which is the BEST food for plants. This way I help to maintain LIFE on EARTH.

I can transform everything that comes from NATURE, in other words everything that is NOT ARTIFICIAL, INTO GOOD THINGS.

ARTIFICIAL things are all those materials that ARE NOT PRODUCED BY NATURE.

When they are thrown away, some of those artificial materials TAKE A LONG TIME to be transformed. This is why it is important to know that THERE ARE DIFFERENT KINDS OF GARBAGE!

Some examples: the leftovers from your snack, the leaves that fall from your mother's plant and the paper from your exercise book are a kind of garbage that is EASY TO TRANSFORM.

But your old sneakers or the toys you no longer play with are a type of garbage that is DIFFICULT TO TRANSFORM, precisely because they are made of artificial materials.

25

There is a very good way to REDUCE that kind of garbage, and that is RECYCLING. This means re-using old materials to make new things.

The PLASTIC from your soda bottle can be used to make a new toy.

The metal from food cans is used again to make new ones.

RECYCLING works well if you SEPARATE THE
GARBAGE! There are COLORED CONTAINERS for that.
There is a special color for each kind of garbage.

Paper Plastic Glass Metal Wood

Dangerous
materials Hospital
waste Radioactive
waste Organic
waste Mixed
waste

So you see, if I am well treated, all the animals, plants and people that need me will be able to live happily and healthily on our beautiful planet EARTH.

ABOUT THE COLLECTION

This Collection is the result of an encounter between two brazilian friends who had not seen each other for more than forty years. One is a biologist, the other an art director and illustrator. Both had the same idea: to combine an amusing text with captivating pictures to make children understand the multidisciplinary questions that arise with regard to the study and perception of the environment. They are driven by the conviction that if we are to protect our planet we have to start working from childhood onwards to change the paradigms.

Israel Felzenszwalb & David Palatnik.

See also the other books from this collection:

CPSIA information can be obtained at www.ICGtesting.com
Printed in the USA
LVIW01n2220250215
428405LV00008B/23